Hopes for Hops

D. L. Morgan

STOCKWELL
PUBLISHERS SINCE 1898

Published in 2022 by
D. L. Morgan
in association with
Arthur H Stockwell Ltd
West Wing Studios
Unit 166, The Mall
Luton, Bedfordshire
ahstockwell.co.uk

British Library Cataloguing-in-Publication Data
A catalogue record for this book is
available from the British Library.
ISBN: 9781399918923

*The views and opinions expressed herein
belong to the author and do not necessarily
reflect those of AH Stockwell*

Contents

This Plastic Paradise. 1
This Town of Steel and Stars 2
Transient Times 4
The Second Self 6
Angled 7
Whither Weather 8
The Coronary Machine 9
Constant Stimulation 10
Rebel Ink 11
Twin Jets 12
From No Side to Full-Time. 13
A B B S S T 14
Retrosexual. 15
Ode to an Imagined Lover 16
Generation Errorists 17
Better Beware 18
Coronach. 19
Cul-De-Sac. 20
Scrap or Scarper. 21
The Bow and Sparrow. 22
The Varieties of Sexual Experience 23
One for Sandra Without Lemon Top 24
Intimations of Immortality. 25
A Typical Day for an Atypical Man 26
Nexistentialism 27
Condemned to Versify 28
Jousting with the Jejune. 29
Pontoon Punter 30
Picayune 31
A Serenade to Sleep – 1. 32
A Serenade to Sleep – 2. 33
She Blows at Every Span 34
Three Times One Table. 35
Haemorrhaging Money. 36
Beyond the Prosaic Prism 37

Residing in the Redolent Realm 38
A Plummet From the Summit 39
Memories of Melancholia 40
Blake, Drake, Lorca and Larkin 41
Incarceration Station 42
Grand Companion – 1 43
Grand Companion – 2 44
Stentorian Sentinels Stand at the Exit Point – 1 45
Stentorian Sentinels Stand at the Exit Point – 2 46
Stentorian Sentinels Stand at the Exit Point – 3 47
An Idiot's Ploy in No-Man's-Land – 1 48
An Idiot's Ploy in No-Man's-Land – 2 49
A Clowder of Cats 50
Once Across a Time 51
Waiting for Deliverance 52
Velocity Exhibition 53
Auguries of Dust 54
Seldom Seen is My Valley 56
A Shilling Shy of Sanity 57
A Reverend's Reverie 58
Altitude 60
A Bottle for the Bogle in the Wood Pogle 61
Initially Yours 62
The Gatecrasher 65
Patterns Emerge 66
That We Might See 67
Valid Air Tax 71
Drinking and Waiting 72
Non Sec Whitter 73
Gerry and Sally Mander 75
The Sonneteer's Serenade 76
There's a Guest in My House 77
Reflections in a Garden High 78
Obituary Attachment 79
The Six Things That Grow Buds 80
The Climate 81
The Seventh Dissipation 82

Hopes for Hops

This book is dedicated to Mair Morgan, Alan Morgan, Gareth Morgan, June Morgan & Leonard Hughes

This Plastic Paradise

I passed a plastic man puffing on a plastic cigarette
Apparently he'd purloined a plastic card to place a plastic bet
The plastic punters on the patio drank from plastic beer glasses
The plastic spectacles on the plastic girl ne'er produced peer passes

A plastic pedestrian produced a plastic phone
Whilst a plastic puppy lay on the plastic pavement prone
The plastic passers-by proffered a plastic shrug
Preposterous be the plastic pleasure of a plastic drug

Plastic pupils peered at a plastic pedalo past the promenade
As plastic priests preached a sermon from a plastic former bard
The plastic plant produced a plastic cloud
As plastic patrons prayed to a plastic shroud

Plastic players poured on to a plastic pitch
Whilst plastic pythons piled into a plastic ditch
Proper plastic promoters prevent plastic being coarse
As plastic golfers pitched up on a plastic course

Perhaps we plastic public should plead for plastic tolerance
As plastic minds predominate plastic political dominance
Plastic lips pout north of plastic breasts
Whilst plastic potters pass over plastic rests

Plastic pounds protrude from plastic pants
As plastic uncles patronise portly plastic aunts
Plastic partygoers praise the plastic as fantastic
Whilst the plastic bungee jumper prays that plastic is elastic

This Town of Steel and Stars

This plant is your plant, and this plant is my plant
From the M4 corridor to Banana Island
A man in a suit in an office with a swipe of his pen
Will to a life of squalor many men condemn

Each man thrills the thing he loves until Gabriel blows his horn
When Golden Handcuffs have been eclipsed by a gauntlet of thorn
A powerful force can be 'The Damned United'
Remember the lyrics from 'The Jam' you cited?

Not all stars are green, but some may well be so
Perhaps there is no heaven, but there sure is hell below
Richard Burton was the first great star of 'Cinemascope'
Before he married Liz, he took the lead in *The Robe*

Thatcher once said 'There's no such thing as society'
The one-trick pony has no concept of variety
A man broken into three-thousand fragments
will see three thousand stars
Yet with closure who will cater for consumer durables and cars?

My grandfather was a foreman, and dad a shop steward
Without industrialisation man is merely a crop hewer
Down the road from my uncles and aunts
lived the young Anthony Hopkins
Dwelling not so far from Ray Milland, Dylan
Thomas and Vernon Watkins

Cameron and his cronies – Old Etonian millionaires
Produce platitudes aplenty but are devoid of cares
An eleventh-hour rescue plan would be something radical
And thus there'd be no need for this plaintive madrigal

The Wizards were at their peak in the twenties and sixties
Giants now replaced by second-rate pygmies and pixies
On the football front there's Port Talbot and Afan Lido
Known across the globe from Sydney to Sligo

Keynes said 'In the future we'll all be dead'
Yet for the present population give us our lead
From the SCOW to BSC and before Tata, Corus
Let Robeson sing among the choir in the chorus

What price now for the homeless hobo?
A man who feels worthless will lose his mojo
Whither the future of the steelworks at Port Talbot?
Where colleagues at the harbour on the boat call 'butt'

Transient Times

I walked out of the museum that was built on a base of Scotch mist
To see a flame-haired woman struck down with a furious fist
Art and life collided like a ten-tonne truck and a bridge
Leaving the victim stranded – cast adrift on a railway ridge

I ploughed on in a state of amnesia, drawing my collar to my chin
And saw a young man in ragged clothing
extracting some food from a bin
The rain marinaded my hair gel, turning my eyes to cruel crimson
I passed a man in a doorway and his friend with prosthetic limbs on

I saw an enraged driver – wielding a finger profanely
As though a thoroughfare owner, acting so pompous and vainly
The lone figures that were passing seemed such an estranged bunch
Is this the state of the nation when it comes to reviewing the crunch?

The smell of fresh food that was frying cut my nostrils to one
The state of my finances forced me to move on by way of a shun
The walk seemed half-eternal with no visible home to alight
What if I was stuck here forever, or at least
the whole goddamned night?

I noticed a couple of beggars, soliciting handouts of cash
A pedestrian would have been run over, save for a momentary dash
The drunkards and swingers collided in a marriage to pain and joy
The Saturday evening crowd has no place for the congenitally coy

The guttural laughter was real, though
leaning sometimes to the forced
None of the folks were thinking of the
Sabbath with its church and roast
The drinkers spilled out on the pavements
in a state of lunacy and lust
The cosmetic paint on the railings was turning rapidly to rust

The genders were mostly divided with communal cracks in between
This is the world in its glory or at least the prodigal scene
Smokers lit up in the gutter on a carpet of discarded butts
A man's face appeared from somewhere
garnished with bruises and cuts

The takeaway outlets were busy as they are at that time of night
The black folks added some colour to the faces ashen and white
Taxi drivers lined up like an army – waiting for battle to commence
Pockets were searched in vainly – where are the pounds and pence?

Kisses were planted as freely, as the wind
shares its sighs with the world
A gentle young woman cries weekly at the sexist abuse hurled
The jokes that are shared are so corny – it's hardly humour at all
The drug user in the back alley is dancing in the death-rattle ball

The Second Self

Do we really need an alter ego?
Down the absent roads that we go?
It's hard enough coping with one – still less two
Who wins when inner peace fights stillness blue?
One need not envy a multitasking actor's rigmaroles
Or watch a documentary about castrated bigger moles
I thought it was the answer – it patently was not
Every heckled stand-up needs a painterly bon mot
If all paths lead nowhere – it's as well to choose one
Hat and cream required to shield the rays of the sun
Patience is a virtue which is its own reward
Absent be the curfew via internal accord
Types abound everywhere – 'arche' and 'stereo'
Each airman owes a debt to Louis Bleriot
So much wasted time – with little progress
Perhaps we all become ensnared with dilettante progress
What of the id, the ego and its super?
Many an invertebrate moves beyond puerile pupa
The renunciation of the will – a noble eastern code
Not every passenger enjoys the feast on board
Donning silly costumes and dyeing greying hair
Does nothing for the six inches lurking under there
Choosing the wrong career for years or even decades
Can only ever result in psychological wreckage
One day a light bulb may be turned on in one's head
Albeit it forty-watt, at least it lights the way ahead
Every voice needs an audience – or even an echo
From the stentorian MP to the last gasp of a gecko
We may be emitting sparks but still need a centre
Some find it by themselves, others need a mentor

Angled

And then it came to pass
Amid small talk
The written word has gravitas

And then it came and went
After a long walk
The money remains unspent

And then it came to light
Among gripping chalk
The beauty of the night

And then I was a dove
Avoiding hawk
The lustful love

And then I rued the past
Angled in baulk
The booze a blast

And then I sailed afar
Across from Cork
The story so far

And then we came together
Admitting stork
The hell of leather

Whither Weather

I love the breeze
It blows dead leaves
Off the highway of life

I hate the rain
It's a bane
And stabs one with a knife

I like the sun
It elevates one
And loves me like a wife

I'm confused by clouds
It's like drunken crowds
Causing strife

I'm not expecting snow
Nor kneading dough
Elsewhere it's rife

What of sleet?
And waving wheat
From Ferndale to Fife

I love the booze
It brings good news
And affirms life

The Coronary Machine

I met a man of twenty-seven who said his best years were behind him
He opined that the three years at university could never be beaten
As a teacher he never rose above the moderate, poor old sinless Jim
Consuming cold crumbs from God's plate, no caviar would be eaten

One can imagine his life panning out, a sad and sorry affair
Forever reverting to type – if not 'stereo' then at least 'arche'
Football on a Saturday, a fortnight's holiday, and grey thinning hair
Only a third of the way through his days, small wonder he was narky

Two point four children and one point eight motor cars
A well-manicured lawn and a painted picked fence
Two hours away from the wife a week, a liege of saloon bars
At sixty-six a heart attack on a foreign field – obituary hence

His friends all said he was a decent chap – with honour to boot
He would be sadly missed by kin and neighbours alike
A moderate will his legacy, so they divided up the loot
His golf clubs sold on e-bay along with fold-up bike

At the age of fifty my life has just begun
There are three echelons – talent, genius and divine
No need now for sleeping pills or else a loaded gun
A mere genius, forever wedded to fine wine

So what of the British equivalent of the American dream?
The hollow man will be sucked into the wasteland of the black hole
The poacher is a fisherman in search of trout or bream
Awake within the titan beyond a Roman mole

Constant Stimulation

I awoke to a breakfast of sunlight and birdsong
Then bathed in caffeine – towelling off with tobacco
Scanning the paper for the daily racing naps
I headed for the cashpoint and more speculation

Passing a man in a car with his middle-market rag
The smell of petroleum and freshly cut grass lifted my spirits
The retail workers smoked alfresco in preparation for the day
As the local eccentrics swam around in the sea of ambivalence

I wondered what my poison would be – grape or grain or Guinness
If there was a meal involved it must be the first
Phone calls would have to be made – family, friends and foe
I reflected that CB and JB shared the same lifespan (1920–1994)

Romance had been retired – like being unchained from a lunatic
There was much to learn from literature and the streets
The first eleven had won but the victory was pyrrhic
Living in the House of Scraps I was king of the paupers

Rebel Ink

Mine is not the rebellion of the biker or fighter
For the pen is truly stronger than the sword
The heaviest thing I pick up is the cigarette lighter
Yet I discovered a belated ability to work the word

Cryptic crosswords and betting slips are just as good
As penning philosophy, poetry or prose
A gallon and a half of ale topped off with fine food
Between her lips I removed an obstructing rose

In the world of modern technology I am a mere Luddite
Forever lapping, lapsing and elapsing
Whether to consume cold cider or else Bud Light?
No longer ungraciously grasping

In truth I had no choice – too ill to work
Iconoclastic to a fault
A malingerer by proxy and prone to shirk
Drinking quality malt

Laptops and computers, texting and tweeting
All alien to me – married to my Biro
An adolescent reader of the words of Adam Sweeting
Empty pockets always waiting for the elusive giro

The fact that I'm out of synch doesn't really matter
As it works so well for me
I have no doubt that ink prevents one from getting fatter
At least in the brain I be!

Twin Jets

The choice is whether to embellish or else pare down
Upon meeting a thing does one look away or in health stare down?
Acting hard is one thing, being so another
Each man deserves a pardon unless he kills his mother

I haven't the faintest idea what the meaning of life is
I guess that's not surprising, since I'm always on the piss
I suppose there's a kind of path that we all meander down
I remember the painted face of the late Amanda Brown

So here I sit in solitude gambling with the muse
Don't mention mental scars, garnished with a bruise
We take recourse to the bottle in times of depression
Leave it twelve hours to the throttle – ossifer's suggestion

To love is to suffer and its absence just the same
Who wants the banality of becoming a Sir or Dame?
Freedom only functions by way of a deposit
We all keep our clothes tucked away in a closet

Every girl gasps below the Sword of Damocles
I'm now an auctioneer so pass the hammer please
In a universe divested of truth, man feels a stranger
All drug addicts drift away or steal a manger

A rolled-up cigarette courtesy of a silver machine
Coming from the town of Burton, Hopkins and Sheen
Come let your hounds dance to the radio
Say to me now that you crave me so

From No Side to Full-Time

It's only death that is truly permanent
Who knows what lies beyond the fiery firmament?
Not everyone can carry the weight of the world
In the full course of time our foibles are unfurled

Yes we drink and smoke but only to the point of gluttony
A black cloud may appear ever so suddenly
One has to make the best of a bad situation
Stranded as we are on this island nation

British people in hot weather are like squid out of water
Who tends now to the adolescent anorexic daughter?
In our beginning is our end and thus vice versa
Who pays now the penniless rhyming verser?

A poem is a town, a village and a city
Who jails now the pillage without pity?
In a few billion years the sun will burn out
The template on the ticket causes few to turn out

A good eight hours' sleep is a boon to the soul
We awake each morning to a breakfast or begging bowl
It's easier to be hurt than to hurt others
No one wants to hide under burnt covers

As the evening blows another final whistle
Another golf ball lost in the gorse or thistle
One more nightcap on the cards or the table
Remember the biblical parable of Cain and Abel?

ABBSST

My face and skin receive communion from the wind gently lapping
No longer at the mercy of absurd person singular clapping
Some people are so poor all they have is money
Remember the boxing world of Jack Dempsey and Gene Tunney

My wallet suffered a heart attack so I gave it the kiss of life
My bank account endured a stroke, denuded by the wife
I see petty little people leading petty little lives
Only the inwardly pretty are perpetually stabbed by knives

Those closest to you will always hurt you the most
Expecting a windfall you'll receive a bill via the royal post
Only sleep and alcohol provide adequate remuneration
A night spent alone and there will be pretty soon elation

People are fucking-ignorant apes, almost without exception
You can expect a kick in the balls when you provide reception
I may miss the sun and booze but don't miss other folk
No use trying to make an omelette minus albumen or yolk

What to do in a world of hate where respite is a stranger?
Maybe regress to a past life or rock away in a manger?
When the time comes to leave, one isn't missing all that much
We think that we are free, but whither the rabbit in that hutch?

As the day is dying the light grows ever more dim
In a way we're lying as night knows sever sore limb
Trust no one and be always vigilant
That's the end for now of my civil rant

Retrosexual

I saw the stars gathering like Hitchcock's *The Birds*
I watched the gunmen slavering as flintlocks absurd
On a light and balmy night anything could happen
In nightclubs up and down the land many a foot was tapping

He who chases monsters shall become one in due course
The scale of wind temperature is measured by Beaufort
You cannot comprehend the magnitude of suffering
Be one from Sandfields, Glanafan or Dyffryn

Ursa Major or Minor, it's all the same to me
Many a racket played, but don't put the blame on me
I sit in splendid solitude contemplating life
As some halfwit plays a tune with a carving knife

Now this night is nearly over, it need not necessarily be repeated
History is generally written by the winners,
so hard luck to the defeated
There is beauty in everything, even the less exalted
The moon imbibed on the horizon as a whisky malted

Now I serve a supper of salad, eggs and ham
Every morning sunrise will surely please a lamb
Do not believe newspapers and their pompous polemicists
Still less invite a jewel thief into your premises

Only buildings leave a shadow, man will soon vanish
Every greedy government seeks to ban and banish
Thank God for the likes of Bacon and Hockney
You're deluded if you think you may con a Cockney

Ode to an Imagined Lover

It's been a full generation since I lived in the land of love
Residing rent-free, a gift gratis before the seraph's shove
When we grew apart it was like being unchained from a lunatic
Someone switched off the power to the drill pneumatic

It's time once again to dust off the tinted spectacles
And throw your old love letters into waste-paper receptacles
Joyous be the sultry sunlight that makes the roses grow
Unhooked from a saline drip that drops the doses slow

Rain your kisses down upon me – on the lips and neck
Rein your reticence in and be liberal with the cheque
I wish to feel the breeze of your breath caress my lonesome cheeks
I could wait a year or decade, but would prefer days or weeks

With whom, where and when in the realm of ribald romance
Doesn't really matter to me, dwelling in the land of no man's
To love is to suffer, but its absence something greater
Roll on the festive feast and tip well the waiter

I was once told: 'It's not how you get them, it's how you get rid'
Yet in the aching auction room I have the brass to bid
Let the aroma of the finest wines be exposed to my palette
Abstinence will not do in the booth of the secret ballot

In some ways I have the patience of a saint, in others the gnat
Bring me my arrows of desire, before I drown in a drunkard's vat
There's not much to declare here, beyond the winsome waiting
A person needs a clear canvas, before they commence painting

Generation Errorists

Imagine describing some non-event as absolutely 'awesome'
Like being a single golfer stuck behind a slow-moving foursome
You may drive invisibly along the motorway in a Sinclair C5
It makes one want to stick one's head inside a sinister beehive

What the hell is a 'power nap'? A nap is a nap is a nap
Conceive of playing for your country and not receiving a cap
'Catch you later' – well you obviously won't because you're emigrating
Nonsensical language like this is more than semi-grating

'Back in the day' implies that the present and the future are obsolete
The melodies of manufactured pop bands are not so sweet
Giving hurricanes names – what is that all about?
Quoting 'Train Crash Tommy' would make relatives' gall stout

Calling Christmas 'Crimbo' as though it was an honorary nickname
Leaves us all in limbo, so we take recourse to a thick mane
Astrology, neologisms and new-fangled nonsense
Come in pretty packages but are devoid of contents

Remember flares in the seventies and mullets in the eighties?
Derelictions of style, nurturing hindsight's gaieties
We now have the 'Premiership', 'Championship'
and leagues one and two
That amounts to four divisions, so who's kidding who?

'Party Seven' and home brew – a drinker's demise
In an effort to be popular we all become unwise
'My autobiography' and a plethora of tautologies
We the preyed-upon public have bought all of these

Better Beware

Gambling on the dogs and horses really is a lottery
Like trying without clay or a wheel to create pottery
Bookmakers produce their profits by betting 'over-round'
Your slice of the cake will thus remain uncrowned

Writers have explored this sport – from Bernard to Bukowski
You know you're in trouble when you can't afford a new house key
One may prefer the flat sprints or the marathons over jumps
The last beast I backed came from the desert with two humps

There'll always be a fair percentage of donkeys and non-triers
Who's that lurking by the stables, armed with pills and pliers?
I have won at two hundred to one and been placed at three hundred
Albeit on a myriad of other sports – on the horses I have blundered

Remember the lessons learnt by the late Dostoevsky
Pity your poor pet when you pass up the cost of vet's fee
It's that damned elusive rush of adrenalin
That we forever seek, regardless of the win

Bertrand Russell wrote 'In Praise of Idleness'
Whether to come on or off the bridle? Stress!
You can bet these days online, via mobile or in shop
Last year's winning tipster has taken a drastic drop

Without inside information we must be ever vigilant
So hard to resist temptation and place a civil punt
Why commit homicide on one's wallet or else purse?
Hear the angry hills echo to the sound of hell's curse

Coronach

I would have enough coin if I stayed out of the pubs and bookies
So now I sit and watch sport, consuming coffee and cookies
Long gone the days when I had to have the last word
I look at life askance on the strength of the absurd

Love for me is fixed firmly in the past tense
Every landowner must erect a first and last fence
One becomes a different person with the onset of middle age
No need to eulogise regarding a feral fiddle's rage

I roll up tobacco via a silver cigarette machine
Edited in nightmares is the fatal car-crash scene
There is a subtle difference between weather and climate
Far from my mind the actions of either primate

I have retained my hair but the waistline is somewhat jovial
In life struggle and pain predominate thus woe be all
Loving literature is news that remains tidings
Does the place still exist that once was called 'Ridings'?

Many take comfort in grass or else the bottle
Give it twelve hours before igniting the throttle
Access to an automobile gives one a sense of independence
Footwear should be appropriate on the acres in the fenlands

Hate can be perfect, like the highest-quality crystal
Most have thought of departure, by means of a pistol
In a commercial world of routine hyperbole
Listen to the busy bees and birds sigh verbally

Cul-De-Sac

I drink in a pub amongst the damned, demented and defeated
It's enjoyable enough but can pall if too often repeated
I reflect upon the wisdom of Arthur Schopenhauer
Whilst embarking on my weekly half a shopping hour

Too much time alone can make a man feel morbid
Taking comfort in my atheism – if I should lose it God forbid
I gave up gambling after my wallet suffered a stroke
I believe I have a conscience just like the next bloke

I continue to smoke despite the health warnings
A roll-up and a cup of tea is how I greet the mornings
Another bloody rainy day can give us all the blues
Seldom seen are good reports in the papers and the news

My car's petrol gauge is never far from the red
I swallow three tablets before and after going to bed
I've run out of credit on my antique mobile phone
Three pennies in my pocket fall short of an ice-cream cone

Whether to bath or to shower – a minor dilemma
Dependent on the season – a no-wonder or remember
My scruffy sideburns are offset by a good goatee
You should see my CD collection – come around and I'll show thee

I scan the obituaries to put a face to a name
Dusting off my old trophies – long retired from the game
Completing a cryptic crossword gives a sense of attainment
As the hands of the clock stop in lieu of payment

Scrap or Scarper

Do not be afraid of the blank page
For it is your opportunity to be a hero
Don't be forever in a rage
Capture the zeitgeist from zero

Most of us by now are tired of Brexit
Within the bureaucratic capitalist system
Whether to stay in or out, enter or exit
These idiots only understand a capitalist's wisdom

Attempts to solve the world's problems
Seldom amount to much
If you can't topple at least wobble 'em
Savour a lover's touch

Pare your life down
To a half-dozen highlights
An eccentric around town
Cameras capture twilight

The canto's crampons will never scale the rock
A warm relaxing bath
Every traumatic event entails an aftershock
For artisan and polymath

The flowing of ink
A boon to the soul
Ermine or mink?
A cultural hole

The Bow and Sparrow

A sparrow sang on an outflow pipe
And the song he sang was 'The Glass of Wine'
In the south of France the grapes are ripe
And in the summer sun we all feel fine

In the beer garden all the benches are full
As the kids splash about in the outdoor pool
A pedestrian curses a motorist
As the sun goes down we all get pissed

At the mercy of the Four Winds
Who will record our daily sins?
As we head home to nightly retirement
The moon in the sky like a bright clear diamond

The Varieties of Sexual Experience

A man may move to Thailand to feast on ladyboys
Each Ann Summers party offers dozens of toys
Every young teenager is ambiguously chaste
Repent at leisure after screwing in haste

There are some sexualities that are beyond the pale
Bestiality and paedophilia not for the hale
Regressing to the safety of the womb or the next best thing
The infantilist throws his dummy out and bonnet into the ring

You may pay for phone sex or want to lay the mother
An addict of asphyxiation may invite terminal bother
The thought of being caught in the act turns a few on
A little death for every lady except the spinster gone

Most masochists don't really want to be beaten
It's having the cake that counts, not the eating
The chronic onanist will experience a draining of energy
Some genuflect in front of a Christlike effigy

What is this modern phenomenon known as dogging?
Orgiastic ecstasy the antithesis of blogging
A blow-up doll offers no emotional response
Forever despised be the imprisoned nonce

Some choose to opt out like the asexual or celibate
The womaniser may cry or conversely celebrate
A sexual partner may not solve the human dilemma
The dog in heat cools down in December

One for Sandra Without Lemon Top

You fell into a black hole and were strung out like spaghetti
Ending up as one of those sculptures by Giacometti
As a philistine you were an addict of the banal
The artist may contemplate jumping into a canal

Blinded by lust and likewise smitten by love
Which one of us now is the bandaged dove?
To see reality one must die and be reborn
Beleaguered be the beast with a perpetual horn

A sufferer in heat awaits the petrichor
Lethal could be an unwieldly petrol saw
You had disdain for those who see through a poetic prism
Empty be the soul garrulous with powder and jism

The majesty of the mob is that they don't really care
For the life of the mind preferring inferior fare
Your warm heart was tainted by the trite
Blue is the coldest colour, painted by the right

They wrote on the will and the unconscious
Schopenhauer and Freud seldom off my conscience
Although I cannot sing, act or draw
I've had my emotions rubbed red raw

They said I had no character and was maybe even yellow
You went to work whilst I read *Herzog* by Bellow
A coming-together and then breaking apart
Tiresome be a life forever dodging a dart

Intimations of Immortality

The voyager to the sublime pauses briefly at bedlam
Even the grandest gourmet will die if he is only fed lamb
Perhaps the world is a cryptic crossword that needs to be solved
Love is just ephemeral and likewise lust never resolved

The astronaut of inner space is the true existential hero
A man is what he does even if he amounts to zero
In a world devoid of meaning one makes one's own truth
From Kierkegaard and Camus right back to the Book of Ruth

Each drinker delights in the dancing of Verity
A good-looking girl with a bob, replete with levity
Most gamblers feel a frisson of pleasure in a loss
Who has not abandoned cream for the divine dross?

Blue, red and yellow – a triumvirate of primary colours
I remember the relatively short life of Carson McCullers
An adolescent godhead may transpire to be a phantom
Every heavyweight champion began life as a bantam

I recall 'Whoroscope' and 'The Genius of the Crowd'
As the world was listening to the words of George O'Dowd
Tranquilised by the trivial. Man ploughs on regardless
The genius trampled on by dog-walkers and gardeners

Both company and solitude are required for sanity
Beauty is a curse but does not preclude vanity
I looked at the Poet Laureate and she at me
I have every admiration for Carol Ann Duffy

A Typical Day for an Atypical Man

I arise before dawn to square up to the new day
Needing tea, tobacco and tablets before I can view play
Driving to the next county to buy the paper and racing form
My wallet takes a deep breath prior to the daily storm

I return home for two hours' study followed by a bath
Whilst listening to the music of The Doors or the 'Stones Aftermath'
I complete a couple of crosswords – cryptic and concise
Gambling alone is better than roulette, craps or dice

After skipping breakfast I drive again to place wagers
Realising that I need a new packet of twin-blade razors
Following lunch I do something decadent but not unmannish
Returning to bed in the manner of the Portuguese or Spanish

A cup of coffee and a cigarette brings me back to the world
Joy or stoicism ensues as the racing results are unfurled
I then read or write in earnest as the night-time beckons
Taking recourse to alcohol for hours, minutes and seconds

Drinking is my greatest pleasure as it opens creative caverns
Imbibing alone or in company in three native taverns
I seldom salute midnight not even on New Year's Eve
When the time comes to turn in, I make no excuses and leave

Martin Amis said that away from writing he
lived 'an average messy existence'
Art and truth are important but of greater value still is persistence
The nature poems of Hughes and Heaney never meant shit to me
In a dream I saw the body of Shelley floating on the sea

Nexistentialism

From whence will come the next great philosophy?
That will illuminate the mindscape and colossal be
The world is as the world does – wars and starvation
Every bride-to-be falls in love with a carnation

It's been a while now but we all need sustenance
The wise man is reluctant to trust in governments
The next grand tome will be welcome and weighty
Who controls now the waters around Haiti?

'God is dead' reported Marx and Nietzsche
The message mutates in the presence of a preacher
Salvaging for crumbs can often terminate in vain
Like watching precious liquid disappear down a drain

Life entails a tapering in body and mind
Who produces the whip in the lobby unkind?
The psyche's been explained but seldom enlightened
Last decade's hero may be next year frightened

We no longer remain seated to applaud a resolution
As advertisements replace literary revolution
The clouds cogitate and the seas are based on the tidal
As we await with our bait for the arid arrival

They say 'Show don't tell' but preferable is the latter
Just as the beer belly of mankind grows hither fatter
It won't be long coming, yet one needs a little patience
The honorary heir of Sartre treats us brittle patients

Condemned to Versify

The road to hell, it is said, is paved with good intentions
And likewise no good deed proceeds unpunished
Many a decent man dispatched in mundane mentions
The single person's flat through a veil of tears unfurnished

You tried to sing for your supper but found yourself tone-deaf
So the plate remained not replete but empty for thee
A gang of basketball giants has no place for the lone elf
The sailor in sunshine will see the skies turn stormy

Each rotund bookmaker welcomes the next mug punter
Into his lair of ludicrous iniquity
Every sensitive poet will find employment as a shunter
And forgo lunch for bureaucrats' high tea

I remember her well in her dress of barbed wire
When she turned her back on yours truly
She dined on a diet of vegan carbon fibre
And lit up joss sticks and patchouli

I roll some more cigarettes courtesy of a silver machine
Thinking of The Beaver and her satirical counterpart
Then pour pints profusely of pilfered poteen
As the old man with the money in his mind mounts a tart

The sultans of small talk and their beloved sultanas
The pursuer of monsters may transpire to be an ogre
Now enough to drive a sane man entirely bananas
See the young woman admire de Beauvoir and yoga

Jousting with the Jejune

Darwin did not kill God
He merely read the eulogy
Likewise Nietzsche did not cull the Creator
He only provided a pew for thee
To contemplate atheism

There's never any austerity for the rich
But the pompous polemicists fail to tell you this
Using sophistry to bolster their arguments
A micturating salesman will sell you piss
To be imbibed at leisure

In an LCD world of petty little men
Society will drag you down
Burning beauty on the bonfire
Forever waving a flag so brown
You know what they've wiped it in

Attempts to govern the world
Seldom amount to much
Even the well-meaning become tainted
From Olympian to crutch
We all must descend the mountain

Crumbs from the high table are better than none
For both the starving and the gluttonous
As a glass of wine will do in lieu of bottle
Always do up a waistcoat one button less
For both paucity and paunch

Pontoon Punter

Some I threw away
Others fell from my grasp
A few were stillborn

Fun to be straight or gay
Unlocked be the clasp
Late at night or early dawn

The boats bob on the bay
Hoarse be the rasp
On the cob sweetcorn

Too many toes of clay
Breathless be the last gasp
Elegant the foal and fawn

Nervous the anorexics who weigh
Chameleonesque the culpable casp
Ian the beast with his horn

Long be the depressive's day
Dangerous the deranged wasp
Lonely the voyeur of porn

Another atrocity on display
Again one failed to grasp
Bereft be the brain of brawn

Picayune

I crawl to life
And life meets me as slowly
And all my pains reside within

You bawl to wife
And wife feels ever lowly
And all your means abide with kin

We fall to strife
And strife deals weather holy
And all our strains applied this skin

She's tall in Fife
And Fife produces goalie
And all her loins untied piss gin

His gall is rife
And rife is roly-poly
And all his reins gift din

They haul in knife
And knife will know Lee
And all their vain shifts win

I stall in life
And life juts out jowly
And all my plans lift fin

A Serenade to Sleep – 1

Behold the man with a cavalier canto in his head
Talking to a fan who saw Chevalier's panto on the Med
Poets are an ugly bunch – piss-poor beyond comprehension
I'd like to kick them in the balls, then abscond from detention

I spent the whole night in Nodsville and slept for seven hours
Not believing in God's will still less heavenly towers
For once there were no noxious nightmares nor abrupt awakening
Resting east of lost west, writers with a block are by day faking

I haven't read a good poem since 'So Now' by Heinrich-Karl Chinaski
Thinking of people without food or clothes, a home or a latchkey
Life came to me quite late – deep in middle age
Dreaming of vodka and crosswords to solve on riddles page

I don't know what's worse, physical or mental anguish
Often they are a married couple and thus a man will languish
Henceforth man resides in an inter-zone without relief
Like a surfer stranded in a rip in a storm upon the reef

Rhyming couplets have been done to death
but worse still is free verse
As a golfer trying to locate his ball in a thicket of furze
I'm now able to enjoy the present and even plan for the future
Just as a wounded person requires a bandage or a suture

Work hard in the diurnal and conversely nightcap the nocturnal
If you're fortunate enough to do this, fate might map the eternal
A packet of cigarettes or else a silver machine for roll-ups
Eschew the denim jacket and forget about your bowl cuts

A Serenade to Sleep – 2

I never had much money, yet was rich in other ways
Not having the manual skills to pitch in brother's gaze
I believe I am the premier poet, save for someone in Asia
Ali was the greatest, Foreman the most ferocious and fearless a Frazier

The reason I say I am the number one is not that I'm that good
It's just that the others are so awful, like actors hewn from wood
I'm not one given to schadenfreude still less to gloating
Only once in my life have I been besotted and doting

I planted a single rose between her luscious lips
And resorted to heavy drinking, and crushing quips
A poem is the whole world, like the streets that make a city
If I'm much mistaken, please feel free to take no pity

I found myself bogged down by the myth of collectivism
Consciousness is what really counts and no less, a vision
One turns to watching films, reading books and hearing music
Perusing the obituary column – the life of an eccentric in a tunic

Man does not kill the thing he loves, his passion destroys him
Where once there were bright lights, it's later dark and dim
Today's revolution will become tomorrow's advertisement
She was only the colonel's daughter but she knew what regiment

Depression destroys the mind, rips out your guts and humour
Like discovering at twenty-one you have a fatal tumour
For those of us lucky enough to survive, drink only to excess
Being good is not enough, just be brave
and bold and to hell with success

Often I've had recourse to a bottle and two pills to slumber
Returning from the racecourse via throttle will not encumber

She Blows at Every Span

The human lifespan is quite enough
So much more would be too tough
See eternity's etude and a heaven in a happy hour
Save for pluvial times, and every seventh visit Paddy Power

If survival is as natural as suffering and woe
Garnish that cigarette with a side order from Bow
Take it from me as a mere man
Slake one's thirst through glass or can

The time has come to take stock and steal
An open window and Adam's ale in widescreen wheel
I prefer pared-down poetry to florid prose
Within my teeth tuck a redolent rose

Those of us lucky enough to leave a legacy
Have experienced being taken down a peg or three
You say it best when you take me from behind
Keep all ends up for the ties that bind

If I may be so bold as to proffer promulgation
The welfare state is the bedrock of any proper nation
The new dawn may not fade if interest is maintained
Visit any backlot and review the rain feigned

Creativity is the crisis of the soul marrying the muse
Every pugilist is familiar with broken bones and bruise
Now this work is nearly over, but there's more yet to come
When you're hounded for wisdom, you have to play it dumb

Three Times One Table

Because I could not wait for time, time paused for me
The tides and the trees are the only treasures free
Like a worm in earth I destroy only my immediate environment
Each man thrills the king he loves – it is his one requirement

Only the inveterately insane tell the complete truth
It's been that way for centuries, since the Book of Ruth
I don't have much time for modern technology
When I was a young man communication was free

I've been a lifelong sports fan and have always loved the arts
The whole effect is much sweeter than the strumming parts
We all have a plethora of pleasure beyond quotidian chores
Like reading about Hammond and Lindrum
or else listening to The Doors

She spent all night in Nodsville, swimming in Blanket Bay
That young girl from Knoxville, in the dying embers of May
She seldom spoke of anything save the changing climate
Befriending a simian priest who rejoiced in the role of primate

When she died we were delivered with a half-page obituary
Oscillating between life and death but now in an ossuary
She made a minor contribution to the literary world
A volume of poetry and short stories, the itinerary unfurled

Some of us find freedom at the bottom of a glass
Or mingling with the great and good via a backstage pass
This really is the end but it need not be terminal
One half of the house espousing Sturm und Drang

Haemorrhaging Money

He often drank two gallons of beer
As he lurched between cheer and tear
Smoking rolling tobacco of dubious quality
Striving for the impression of curious jollity

His lovers had all left him like the ebb tide leaves the shore
His bank account cried out 'No Mas' or else no more
He took an axe to the box labelled 'Christmas Fund'
Envying the financial wherewithal of the businessman

With a philosophy that never stretched beyond 'Carpe diem'
He could be found betting on the fortunes of Marcel Siem
Eschewing both track and field and forsaking the gym
He wished that his wallet would pray or sing a hymn

With no credit in his phone and petrol gauge in the red
He abandoned the idea of a retreat instead
Having single-handedly paid for mug's villa on the hill
His father knew both Joe Coral and William Hill

He saw the bottom of a bottle via borrowed cash
He found a pyre and set light to his dwindling stash
In the cold light of day he still could not comprehend
Why he spent so much time with a pompous friend

We all need human rights for responsibility is boring
Why not leave home and go on a pub crawl touring?
What happens when there's no money for another measure?
We imbibe in haste and reproach ourselves at leisure

Beyond the Prosaic Prism

Margaret Thatcher was not a conservative
In a confined space convert to live
Neither was Scargill a unionist
He could not be as many pissed

Gore Vidal told me who killed John Kennedy
As related via big brother Bennady
A lover's caress won't last forever
From tiny Tim to intrepid Trevor

Castro gave a home to Mercader
Persecuting gays who lived life harder
Touching from a distant shore
Within five seconds flat out on floor

Gunboat diplomacy from Lord this or that
Watch the grace of a lissom cat
All political systems are bad but some are worse
Overlooking psychology – the leftist's curse

Trotsky honeymoon serenade the naked
Take a potato, add cheese and bake it
Drink a drink of new origin
Whisky, vodka, Drambuie or gin

Machiavellian machinations maintained to this day
Yes, Prime Minister a classic for the ages not feet of clay
I don't want the truth I want something to write to people
Church not made with hands without spire or steeple

Residing in the Redolent Realm

In the kingdom of the myopic
We sing songs on any topic
Somewhere south of that tropic
Imbibing copiously from an opaque optic

Lubrication can pave the way
A refuge from the bloody fray
Every night and much of the day
Looking for elusive prey

Each dreadful day time's arrow flies
Within the hand a narrow pliers
Before noontide the dewdrop dries
Forgotten now heroic fliers

Astronauts of inner space
A marathon of a single pace
Emerging from a veil of lace
Painting patterns on the grail of grace

A released emotion – a captured frame
Refracted from the glass-bead game
The feral lamb and the leonine tame
A barrister beyond bluster and blame

Raise a glass before thy doom
A bed for you weaving loom
Dolly out and inward zoom
Postpone now the time of tomb

A Plummet from the Summit

One sups upon the Tyne
And one across sublime
A compulsive cruciverbalist
Not long after noontide half pissed

Once below so fine
Imbibing a rich red wine
Something savoury for dinner
Elusive be the competition winner

Fifty-four seconds my all-time record
As I began renovating the lime decor
Seventy-five crosswords in a single morning
An afternoon of vodka that greets the dawn in

What are normal people doing?
Pots of tea brewing?
Bringing up the issue?
Wiping tears with tissue?

Tobacco an ever-present – a necessary evil
Light work the life of a secretary devil
Sunlight so elusive in these pluvial parts
Banter thrown around as jovial darts

A book a film a CD
An existence somewhat seedy
Rolling up the Rizlas
Is 5 down 'business'?

Memories of Melancholia
(Original Version)

I awoke to open the curtains – Dralon and crimson in hue
As the sun took out a tissue and relieved the grass of its dew
I had found a house in the country, a semi-rural secluded retreat
Wrongly thinking that a young man's life precluded defeat

I took a decade's sabbatical from the thriving, thrusting throng
And immersed myself in the world of elegiac art and song
It was night for day and frost in the middle of summer
The emotional drains were blocked with no sign of a plumber

I existed mainly on a diet of jacket potatoes and cheese
Where the only spontaneous thing that I
did was emit a sibilant sneeze
I had left my place of employment by mutual consent
The past was then part of my present – what
ruse would the future invent?

Depression feels somewhat like an out-of-body experience
The pounds came tumbling off, so what hope for the weary pence?
Would I ever regain my place in the resonant human race?
As I looked longingly at the rope or at least the lengthy lace

When it's raining in your head, the outset is of little comfort
I often checked my pulse to discover a brittle drum port
How long would it last – and could I find the right medication?
Trying everything from analysis and booze to night meditation

All the masts had been taken down by a rabid naval crew
You find yourself cursing the hearse and the natal too
Despair doesn't just scramble your brain,
it rips out your entrails plenty
The worst feeling in the world is that life is futile and empty

Blake, Drake, Lorca and Larkin

The four best poems of the twentieth century?
The Waste Land
'Fern Hill' especially the last two lines
'The Genius of the Crowd'
With 'Howl' completing the suite

Talent, genius and the divine are yet to mention me
There's much I can't stand
Not 'dark satanic mills' accompanied by white wines
'Tyger tyger' nocturnally prowled
A bowl of cawl followed by a sweet

Persistent rains in the principality drenches me
'Nick Cave and the Bad Seeds' the optimum band
Avoiding speed traps but penalised by five fines
No pounds in the pockets of a shroud
Waving wistfully Van Gogh's fields of wheat

An undiscovered genius from China will
rule the twenty-first century
A breath of cool wind across the face fanned
The closure of steel plants and a multitude of mines
'One more take, Bob' JH growled
Remember the modernists, Morrisons and beat

What remains of us is not love but a legacy of lust
A legendary Lorca now a handful of dust
When spoilt for options one may be nonplussed
Hughes and Heaney were nonchalantly not fussed

Incarceration Station

So there I was sitting in the back of a CID squad car
Having been arrested for imbibing too much lemonade and vodka
Apparently I had offended the sensibilities of an elderly spinster
And a northern reverend on parole from his minster

I felt as Gregor Samsa in the grip of a police state
Or an overworked hamster in the trip on a goalie's wait
Time turned backwards or at least remained static
I thought of the toys that I played with contained in an attic

With no money to afford a lawyer or to stand bail
I was looking at twenty years in solitary in jail
Human rights are sometimes pretty low on the totem pole
Dead industry may be beautiful but no longer floats on coal

Denied a single phone call it was an introduction to qualms
A flat battery is no use to early morning alarms
What would the papers write if they knew the story
Whether left-leaning, liberal or purely Tory

We all travel alone, though we may have many friends
A pound sometimes appears when the penny ends
Do not rest at leisure when your liberty's at issue
No use in a wet thing called a tear so eschew the tissue

All things are sent to test us so we should not be surprised
My good luck had run its course I inwardly surmised
So here I sit in limbo with neither food nor bed
The unjustly imprisoned citizen feels as good as dead

Grand Companion – 1

I met him on an evening of beer and beef curry
Words were shared in the blear of brief hurry
Telephone numbers were exchanged – landline then
Twenty-three years later I take a grand fine pen

I had just split with my girlfriend, and lost my job
Also being declared bankrupt, a sad frosty yob
Four months in a mental hospital closed the picture
A full complement of nasties – overdosed mixture

Initially the relationship was somewhat romantic
Yet I was uptight then – neurotic and pedantic
Things then progressed to the plateau of the platonic
Just as Blondie's best song was probably 'Atomic'

Trust was built slowly – via wine and fine dining
In a village once renowned for the industry of mining
Most of our time was spent indoors
He listening to Ken Colyer and me The Doors

A love of newspapers – obituaries and sport
Maybe a cheeseboard garnished with port
My constant smoking pissed him off
I gave up for six month after a hissing cough

He is a generation older than me – but I love history
Chemistry an enigma – an unknown quantity
The would-be poet and the distinguished member
When I lived on the margins he was my centre

Grand Companion – 2

Pansexuality is small fry compared to mental health
Some people are so poor all they covet is wealth
The decades wore on but companionship thrived
Until one day good cheer for both of us arrived

Me the gambler, drinker and smoker
The smouldering embers stirred by a poker
A quarter of a lifespan has elapsed into history
Gone but not consigned to the malaise of mystery

Who knows what the future holds but today's not so bad
Winter grips water within its frozen plot of land
Many a late night spent drinking and talking
Watching cue-ball wizards in the arena chalking

I made so many mistakes but can't dwell in the past
Who would have thought that the years could pass so fast!
The sail soars serenely in the sun at full mast
If the first quarter was a calamity, the second a blast

Now this poem is nearly over we may not know its value
If only I'd followed the advice of the insights that gal knew
When I am tired I rest upon a pew
The big bang fired – the crest shone anew

Stentorian Sentinels Stand
at the Exit Point – 1

I remember your sequined see-through blouse
That you wore for all the world to observe
The Glorious Twelfth not so good for grouse
A world alien to the realms of reserve

Once again you beat me ruthlessly to love
With the aid of your seminal second serve
An answer refused to be resolved from above
So we must regain aplomb and hold out our nerve

I tried to solve the mystery of your labyrinthine psyche
Again to no avail as we parted soon after
You wore some kind of leisure outfit advertising Nike
At least you left me with issue and laughter

We clashed like titans and parted like the Red Sea
Memories are made of much including the mystic
Your love alone for half a decade forcibly fed me
Crosswords are enjoyable concise but better still cryptic

What are you doing now – I dare say married?
It must be a quarter of a century since we last met
I wish you well and hope you have not miscarried
Remember dragging me out of the off-
licence and refusing to sub a bet

Stations of the Cross need not be terminal
A man must respect rapport and create a system
We saw *Jean De Florette*, *Manon des Sources* and *Germinal*
If there is no God to genuflect, to worship wisdom

Stentorian Sentinels Stand
at the Exit Point – 2

A relationship is a war zone but there are times of truce
Solitude is preferable to perpetual strife and struggle
I seldom took a single point off you, let alone reached deuce
I don't want no habitual wife's bland cuddle

We were both addicts but neither needed to score
Often frequented were galleries of sandpaper and glue
As you aged your animation transformed to snore
Remember rectilinear Mondrian maintaining primary hue

The one holiday we took turned out to be a disaster
Work is only a means to an end and interminable drudgery
When I returned for a season I remained in plaster
Not being inclined to hug, still less to touch a tree

We shared a love of music but repetition kills everything
Fields may be soggy or else Elysian
The multitude are ingrates just bill any king
No use playing a round in a storm or even a breezy one

Political systems seldom work once office is attained
Thank the ages for alcohol garnished with tobacco
An open marriage is no better than one that's been arranged
You may creosote the fence varnished with lacquer

My career ascended as both gambler and writer
For age gives one a greater understanding of proportion
I recall relatives calling me a useless blighter
Even the humblest dogsbody may one day earn promotion

Stentorian Sentinels Stand
at the Exit Point – 3

The suffering of the world is too much for a soul to bear
Stentorian sentinels stand at the exit point
It's not that we pay it no mind or don't fully care
Covid-19 superseded the tedium of another Brexit joint

The history of the world proves that man's natural state is war
Dignity is only won by years of intelligent effort
A liberal sees too many grey areas thus has nothing to want for
Everything changes its spots aside from the leopard

Few of my heroes were physically attractive
Each man thrills the queen he shoves
Pensive be the passive person and alive the active
Standing for hours before steely stoves

The roads are best traversed in splendid isolation
A hot shower or a bubbly bath a joy to behold
What is to be done to mend this island nation?
Hair should be washed if not daily, weekly three-fold

There's more truth in a day's newspaper other than the politics
Than a million novels or lukewarm verse
Whether to live in a town or a city or else out in the sticks
Do not walk in wild weather or fight through furze

You cannot have light without contrasting darkness
Families don't fuck you up but they like to put the boot in
In every fine face lines mark stress
The world is governed now by apologists for Trump and Putin

47

An Idiot's Ploy in No-Man's-Land – 1

At sixteen I travelled beyond the trappings of religion
Which seemed about as weighty as the droppings of a pigeon
I fell under the spell of Marx, Engels, Lenin and Trotsky
What of the legacy? The fall out at Chernobyl
and pennings of Chomsky

A revolutionary nutter who failed to understand human psychology
Not having read Darwin or comprehending basic biology
Time changes most things and for that we should be grateful
The human heart can be sublime but also houses the hateful

Love arrived late but so much better than never
I fondly remember Tracy looked after by Dan Trevor
The nine-to-five did not appeal – I could not stand the snail's pace
Losing all appetite for food I could no longer say grace

There were many sporting heroes and also a love of music
Dressing up in daft costumes – tank top, tabard and tunic
I hated poetry – especially Gerard Manley Hopkins
Barely knowing who Dylan was let alone Vernon Watkins

'Tis not folly to be wise for ignorance is a curse
Every man waxes his wallet, every woman her purse
I found the key to my life at the age of fifty-two
Lacking social skills and responding stiffly too

The future cannot be as bad as the blighted past
Not always a great picture made by a knighted cast
Do not sink to strategies and categories condemned
The blood that flows inwardly should externally be stemmed

An Idiot's Ploy in No-Man's-Land – 2

Exchange all heroes for spirits of a different sort
Who when bribed by a billionaire cannot be bought?
The man who fears death is really scared of life
In wartime even the craven must be prepared to knife

I was never young and easy in the way that Thomas was
Yet having to renounce angst for the knack of common cause
You may wander through the world and yet remain aloof
Everyone needs a hot meal and warm bed
and hear rain upon the roof

If you cannot change the world at least redeem the self
Yet the inner titan may emerge from the embryo of an elf
If I serenade you would I receive ale and alms?
Let us be as one and believe in rails charms

Now this poem is nearly over who knows what it means?
Be forever vigilant and forsake the furies and fiends
Many a slip discovered after the anchor has been lifted
John, James and Jane jaundiced or just jilted?

A Clowder of Cats

If cats could talk what would they have to say to us?
As we lift up heavy shopping and clamber on the bus
A tame or feral feline is a master unto himself
Likewise the mistress, consuming bird off the shelf

They watch us in the kitchen stirring oriental herbs
As they reach for the speech and vouch for the verbs
With fur as smooth as silk and a tail so splendid
As the broken bookshelf in the lounge lies unmended

They are lords of the lawn and ladies of the night
Prowling on their beat under a blanket of moonlight
They must mention us and together conspire
As we extinguish the flames and for the night retire

A saucerful of milk to greet the break of dawn
Some edibles to boot – may tuna and sweetcorn
They have a sense of independence unlike most dogs
Sleeping by the fire and lapping up the logs

Perhaps they're filing a report to be handed in to office
A weekly meeting convened – purring in the coppice
There's not much to declare here – beyond human folly
Whilst we adorn our homes with mistletoe and holly

Now this poem's nearly over but what does it really mean?
Perhaps we wish to penetrate the clandestine feline scene
They dominate us rather than vice versa
The same the world over from Miami to Merthyr

Once Across a Time

Once abreast a time there were three Christian names
J. P. R. Williams and T. G. R. Davies two kings of oval games
The summer of '76 parched the grass to brown
One year later some folks celebrated the jubilee crown

Once across a time a nation did so well
In a much-derided decade now demoted to hell
Reardon, Griffiths and Mountjoy won everything on the baize
As kipper ties and flared trousers were the latest craze

Once askance a time the leaders were less right wing
Taylor and Burton now no longer queen and king
The miners went on strike and there was a three-day week
Is the emblem of a nation a daffodil or a leek?

Once along a time the seasons were delineated
The life of the child is continuously animated
Stuart Evans wrote of 'The Caves of Alienation'
A conservative in a predominantly socialist nation

Once above a time Lord Lucan disappeared
Perhaps residing in Goa with a long and straggly beard
Alan Evans won 'The News of the Word'
and Leighton Rees 'The World'
The principality was the focus for the best arrows hurled

Once astride a time Rachel Roberts took a *Picnic at Hanging Rock*
Geoff Wheel and Allan Martin a powerful combination at lock
The punk-rock explosion shook up a staid scene
The adult atheist then prayed green

Waiting for Deliverance

So here I am, waiting for something musical or novel
Dwelling in a place neither a palace nor a hovel
Enjoying the freedom of an extended furlough
Reading my newspaper and drinking a fine Merlot

We cancelled a fortnight's holiday in a Swiss chalet
The airfare was too expensive let alone a valet
Science is reductivist but the arts are ennobling
Imagine expecting Mozart only to hear some arsehole yodelling

Sometimes I feel like other folks are as a praying mantis
Wishing that they'd disappear in the manner of Atlantis
Blessed is the realm of the ascetic scholar
As the world outside fights over a single dollar

Perhaps I drove down one too many a cul-de-sac
Maybe the foreign fisherman sailed to Hull and back
Every relationship always includes the binary
As you dressed down on Friday eschewing all finery

Each day involves a test with paper litmus
The red and blue parties check our political fitness
Your thick skin was really rather porous
As the obituary columns herald the final chorus

We try to swim the waters but are engulfed by a sluice
Whisky and vodka respectively with coke or orange juice
The world will keep on turning until the sun burns out
How can you stay with a man who daily earns nowt?

Velocity Exhibition

Physically I've had an easy life not having joined
the army or worked down a mine
My toughness comes from the ability to down three bottles of wine
At one sitting and still being able to stand
Communing with the gods – Dionysus so grand
Chain-smoking at leisure does little for the lungs
My ladder to fitness – now devoid of rungs
Good health will never deliver immortality
The world looks very different from a porthole at sea
One thing I have not done is travel the globe
It may widen the wisdom but brings the comfort of Job
Most men are unable to sit and cogitate
They need the adrenalin rush each and every date
Freedom is not all it's cracked up to be and neither is sex
Remember the fate of the once mighty T-Rex
One day they'll tax the air and force us to pay
A pollution policy that will never go away
A corpulent cat in the garden prowls upon his beat
Before basking in the sunshine and absorbing the heat
Television's at its best in the standby mode
Such drivel and detritus beamed into our abode
Uninterrupted sleep a necessary respite
I like to sit by the window in the best light
I often measure out my days in terms of rolled tobacco
Walking along the high street the nostrils parley with tabasco
The ugly business of sledging spoils modern cricket
There's no need to humiliate a man after he's lost his wicket
There can be no joy without sorrow or remorse
Many a tee shot will bypass the fairway for the gorse
Everything that comes to pass must be evanescent
Only a halfwit is permanently effervescent
Today's married couples will be tomorrow's divorcees
What is eternity, but the mountains and the seas

Auguries of Dust

A man may wish to paint a scarlet mural
After spending the night with a harlot rural
The archetypal conservative appears to be cussed

Every woman is obliged to spend much time on her appearance
As the shop's greatest sale will be the final clearance
The communist is well aware of economic boom and bust

All people must undergo suffering – physical and mental
Such as anxiety, earache and the agonies of the dental
The nationalist believes the foreigner to be little more than rust

The drug user's countenance may appear to be ashen
The teenager will be tormented by unrequited passion
The apolitical man in the system has no trust

The pre-race horse is paraded in the paddock
The fisherman in his trawler hunts herring and haddock
The liberal sees the grey area and will be trapped and trussed

The crowd will notice the albino's different pigment
Reality is grounded but the imagination sometimes a figment
The fascist philosophy is one of bloodlust

The bereaved widow may entomb the ashes
As the international news highlights inevitable clashes
The nihilist is aware that we all return to dust

The middle-aged man could be coarse and corpulent
Envious be the poor of the orbit of the opulent
The anarchist believes in peeling away constitutional crust

The adolescent speculates on what lies beneath the bodice
The nurturing mother lives a different life to the sex goddess
Abandoning socialism in the Labour Party discussed

The independent may involve himself in the petty local
The magnate sits and schemes on a settee global
The environmental campaigner believes his cause is just

Seldom Seen is My Valley

Residing as I am in the Dulais Valley
I sit and watch the darts on TV from the Ally Pally
I choose to cross the county border for purposes retail
Living next door to a pub it's hard to recall detail

The garden proffers a hearty salutation to the morning sun
A policeman on his beat is the uniformed warning one
There is very little trouble unlike the village north
No Vikings or marauders to plunder the pillage forth

There is something timeless about a hamlet's hallmark
The rugby players train in the evenings on the ball park
The Furies and the Norns can't locate this on a map
The international too modest to display his honoured cap

No coastal breezes here nor the city's pace
The comedian in the club a wise and witty ace
A bus stop and a call box garnish the roadside lay-by
Two friends across the street exit and sadly say 'Bye'

There's an elegiac quality to late industry
To see the pit closed down causes heartfelt injury
How can the service sector succeed when there's little money?
The bees are buzzing around yet small signs of honey

The mountains still stand proud if somewhat weather-beaten
Someone's moved in next door by the name of Heather Keaton
If the bombs do not explode there'll be another millennium
The landline phone is ringing – it's Uncle Bill Kenyon

A Shilling Shy of Sanity

I summoned up the necessary gratitude
For the motorist who let me through
I wish I had more than a platitude
I give hereby to you

I saw the barber's BMW – but I tipped him anyway
Viewing the watercolourist's blue
Pity the poor man who never gets his end away
Chatting amiably we form an orderly queue

The food was awful yet I gave the girl a gratuity
As the sun wiped away the morning dew
Such small portions in lieu of annuity
We walked into a bar and bought the local brew

The taxi driver took the scenic route
A potter who could barely see to cue
I heard the moans from within the boot
As the meter made a wallet stew

Perhaps we're all a shilling shy of sanity
The mountain wears a belt of mist around its verdant hue
Living in a fantasy world of obverse vanity
Your appointment has been cancelled, due to doctor's flu

So what of this thing we loosely call society?
Apart from technology there's presently little new
No escape for the man in permanent sobriety
Despite our ideologies we should feel brittle too

A Reverend's Reverie

May the good gods give grace to every mother and daughter
That they might drink copiously from cups of clear water
Let it be known that age gives one a great sense of proportion
As every manager seeks the title or at least promotion

I think I'm in the top five poets of eternity's pantheon
It's not that I'm that good but others are the opposite of champion
May we celebrate the lives of those who chose to change gender
The future is unwritten, so we look forward to a novel agenda

I was only granted peace of mind when others are turning in
Perhaps crystal blue cut glass alleviates brutal burning skin
It's true that most political systems seldom seem to work
Just as the men of apparent wisdom transpire to be jerks

May you be free of famine, physical pain and mental hurt
The lover of soft fabrics feels estranged in a metal skirt
Why is there so much suffering, agony and lingering death?
Free speech and fine food should be a
staple diet until the final breath

The helping hand is so much better than the cruel iron fist
Just as the dunes of sand grow higher until one is too pissed
Brevity is the mother of each newborn spontaneous wit
Every person who's out of shape envies the physique of the fit

If politics and religion leave a person cold,
turn to the philosophy of old
You may prospect for bronze and silver so a bonus is finding gold
We cannot imagine the suffering of the victims of the Holocaust
The nineteenth hole that we imbibe in, is
a comparatively hollow course

Most young people undergo a period of prolonged pain
But as day follows night, sunshine must be the heir of rain
Edward and Lead Foot seldom understood
that you can't have dark without light
The person you think of as a dullard with
the passage of time is truly bright

There are poets of the page, canvas and musical scores
Inevitably in a bar you find yourself seated beside bores
Yet let us not judge others for they have skills we do not possess
Is there anything more sensual than wearing
your wife's white wedding dress

If you can deconstruct this verse you're a better human than me
The length of a film should only list the time it takes to pee
There's nothing wrong with gambling, drinking and various vice
Round off a late evening with a chicken curry and rice

Altitude

I remember your black beret
That you wore at an angle
And all who lived within
Eros
Cupid
Borgias
Rabelais
Casanova
And others whose names escape me
Your love for me
Stemmed not from what you desired
But what you failed to hate
An uninvited guest must make the best of what he finds
Therefore
I became
Your humble servant
And you my mistress of the nocturnal
And the diurnal
Transported to an interstellar galaxy
Once spotted a thousand miles west of Venus
Travelling not alone
But coupled
As a gin and tonic
You wearing emerald
Both the colour and the jewel
Not for ostentation
Yet perhaps subtly so
Then one day the air became too thin
So you took off your mask
That you had worn
And left me
This poem

A Bottle for the Bogle in the Wood Pogle

Come fill up your glasses of brandy and wine
Imbibe whisky and vodka and forever feel fine
Beer and cider should be drunk by the gallon
Sit for a while on the banks of the Shannon

We don't need drugs just the drug of us
Squeeze every pour but pass over the pus
Every decanter should be eternally replete
Without a glass in a man's hand his life is incomplete

Be it supermarket, off-licence or pub
Or perhaps a ladies' and gentlemen's club?
Maybe I should write a sonnet?
Or look at the water lilies of Monet?

This sure ain't Shakespeare
But who gives a toss?
Lend me a tenner
And I'll show you who's boss!

For the guts and gore of Gallipoli
I reluctantly fall happily

Initially Yours

S. E. Hinton's work was a kind of 'Camus for Kids'
There's no record now if she's prospering or on the skids
A. E. Housman professor and poet penned *A Shropshire Lad*
The elder brother of the writer Laurence and seldom a cad

The prolific P. G. Wodehouse exercised his wit on golf
I was introduced to his work by my ex-colleague Rolf
An influential English post-war novelist was J. G. Ballard
Whose dystopian prose resembled the majesty of 'The Mallard'

Who remembers now the ghost stories of M. R. James?
As work continues apace along the banks of the Thames
Christopher Robin became immortalised by way of A. A. Milne
Every drinker should give thanks to the invention of the kiln

The American H. P. Lovecraft wrote some very weird tales
As the dismissed batsman bemoans the loss of his bails
The original author of *A Fairytale of New York* was J. P. Donleavy
One time friend of Brendan Behan – a noted drinker and heavy

The Waste Land is the masterpiece of the late T. S. Eliot
Who had no need for a pseudonym unlike George Eliot
If an inspector calls to your home you'll think of J. B. Priestley
No relation to the twice world champion
Dennis 'The Menace' Priestley

The less famous Welsh Thomas rejoiced in the initials R. S.
Who lived so far away from the literary scene in Paris
e. e. cummings was more than effective in lower case
An Ivy League scholar and poet and painter of grace

J. D. Salinger lived the life of the literary recluse
The Catcher in the Rye still a popular peruse
W. B. Yeats won the Nobel Prize and wrote 'Easter 1916'
His brother Jack B. a painter familiar with the colour green

J. K. Huysmans was a major influence on Wilde
Encompassing a decadent world that often beguiled
C. L. R. James saw very far beyond the boundary ropes
A Marxist activist who had little time for popes

R. M. Ballantyne was the Scot who gave us *Coral Island*
A great joy in childhood on this amoral island
Critical opinion is divided in the case of D. H. Lawrence
Seven Pillars of Wisdom the war work of T. E. Lawrence

A master of form and content was the poet W. H. Auden
A far less ignominious life than that of General Gordon
R. D. Laing a brilliant psychiatrist and Scottish alcoholic
Met his end on a tennis court and would no more frolic

R. D. Blackmore wrote extensively including *Lorna Doone*
Maybe financially he was born a century too soon
The undisputed master of misanthropy was H.-G. Clouzot
Whose coruscating films leave a man reaching for ouzo

The title of an L. P. Hartley book was adopted by an Australian band
We're all go-betweens now in need of a well-dealt hand
Was there ever a batsman with a greater aura than I. V. A. Richards?
It seemed as though everyone else had dined on mere pilchards

Subtle was the work of E. M. Forster
In contrast to the adventures of C. S. Forester
Beau Geste overshadows all other work by P. C. Wren
Writing several centuries after the life of Aphra Behn

The greatest tackler of all time has to be J. P. R. Williams
Who dovetailed so well with his namesake J. J. Williams
S. J. Perelman wrote prodigiously including for the brothers Marx
Living in the land of the heroine Rosa Parks

There was more to the life of G. K. Chesterton than Father Brown
A larger-than-life character and wit-around-town
A. S. Byatt is the elder sister of Margaret Drabble
I would not like to compete against either of them at Scrabble

J. M. Synge was a fine dramatist who died before forty
Writing *The Playboy of the Western World* but never himself haughty
H. L. Mencken was a polymath who attacked the bourgeois
V. S. Naipaul a stimulating author to be read upon the sofa

JFK's head exploded on the fateful Dallas day
Mystery still surrounds operations at 'The Bay'
Many a youth enjoyed the yarns of Captain W. E. Johns
Whilst later generations simply sat and watched the Fonz

C. P. Snow united two seemingly disparate cultures
As the wounded soldier is always in need of sutures
P. D. James remains popular even in her nineties
A half-round of golf only requires nine tees

A. J. Cronin gave us the world of *The Citadel*
Some kind of relief from the realm of bitter hell
A lover of legends and science fiction was the novelist T. H. White
He would have approved had he lived of the sportsman Jimmy White

The greatest English landscape painter has to be J. M. W. Turner
Living some time before German *Nosferatu* director F. W. Murnau
One of the Kings of the short story was H. E. Bates
The Darling Buds of May et al still selling in crates

H. G. Wells died just after the war
A visionary who questioned life before
Many have fallen for the charms of J. K. Rowling
No doubt Harry Potter is now grown up and growling

A fervent champion of Darwin was biologist T. H. Huxley
Whose grandson wrote *Brave New World* one Aldous Huxley
F. R. Leavis placed literature and culture under scrutiny
If he read something he didn't like he was inclined to mutiny

J. R. R. Tolkien wrote about Bilbo Baggins and Frodo
Seeking out the darkness that was the land of Mordor
Oxford and television were the homes of A. J. P. Taylor
But now it's time to fix that dodgy derailleur

The Gatecrasher

What we leave as legacy
Ricochets through eternity
The truth that beggars see
Outweighs the cant of Colonel T.

Nature is best viewed from a distance
Light and dark needed both for perspective
What becomes of the Tysons, Foremans, Listons?
A shrug of the shoulders in response to invective

I beat those beautiful bastards in terms of time
Albeit ephemerally before one's Maker
Do not dilute lager with lukewarm lime
A plot is enough, there's no need for an acre

Even Gary Player now has a paunch
The teenage years last longer than the rest
A stalwart must be steadfast and staunch
Grateful should be the gatecrashing guest

I was once in love
With Karen Elizabeth Austin
A girl who called out the dove
And never let frost in

Although it's no more
The feeling remains
Exposed is the pore
The gods live in details

Patterns Emerge

There is a certain type of guy – burly, bellicose, banal
That makes one yearn for the deepest cold canal
Very large of physique but the adverse of brain
I guess it's been this way since the time of Cain

Vacant vessels always vocalise belligerent
Superficial, reactionary and generally ignorant
It's as though a conversation is a sparring match
One has to be fleet of foot to avoid a cutting clatch

The hawk of schadenfreude is circling in the air
If you're looking for respect then you'd better beware
Crashing bores everywhere that intrude upon your time
Making you feel like a culprit despite the absence of crime

They may be loosely termed the 'lumpen proletariat'
It's the same the world over – a jumping stolen lariat
They've always behaved in a certain way and will continue to do so
Not the kind of social contract envisaged by Rousseau

The best way of dealing with trouble is to avoid it
An old Chinese proverb before the work Jung and Freud did
There is another path – albeit one hard to locate
Cross the street from the pavement of the puerile po-face

They had doors of perception slammed in their face
Or at least the key taken away
Condemned to live a life of disgrace
And sit and suffer in lieu of a better way

That We Might See

Would that a fisherman never make another catch
Would that a locksmith not find a new latch
Would that a copper make no more arrests
Would that a landlord take in no guests
Would that a tobacconist sell no cigarettes
Would that a bookmaker take no more bets
Would that a mechanic work no second-hand cars
Would that a wino find no more bars
Would that a swimmer fail to locate waters
Would that a father not see his twin daughters
Would that a priest take no more prayers
Would that a stallion cover no mares
Would that the junkie not get the next fix
Would that a magician forget all his tricks
Would that an athlete break both his legs
Would that the chicken lay no more eggs
Would that the matches all end in draws
Would that the whore reclaim her drawers
Would that the builder lose his best trowel
Would that the consonant not marry the vowel
Would that the burglar lose all of his loot
Would that the potato grow with no root
Would that the prizefighter lose both of his gloves
Would that the pacifist lose sight of his doves
Would that an actor forget all his lines
Would that the fork come with no tines
Would that the tree not have a bark
Would that the night never be dark
Would that the nurse have no one to tend
Would that the insurer have no money to lend
Would that the teacher have no child to scold
Would that the knight no longer be bold

Would that the grave contain no bodies
Would that the army were devoid of all squaddies
Would that the singer lose their golden voice
Would that the voter have not a choice
Would that the driver lose his steering wheel
Would that the orange come with no peel
Would that the television have not a picture
Would that the Saturday hold not a fixture
Would that the grass no longer be green
Would that a miser forget he was mean
Would that the reactionary have no political aim
Would that the caged animal no longer be tame
Would that the comedian forget all his gags
Would that an urchin discard his rags
Would that the kettle have no water to boil
Would that an engine leak all of its oil
Would that the gangster lose his best moll
Would that a girl lose her pet doll
Would that the chef have nothing to cook
Would that the library hold not a book
Would that the rain no longer be wet
Would that the borrower be no more in debt
Would that the soldier make no more kills
Would that the fish survive without gills
Would that the judge have no one to sentence
Would that the rueful have no repentance
Would that a bird no longer have wings
Would that the wedded never swap rings
Would that the pen contain no ink
Would that the kitchen have not a sink
Would that the sun were no longer yellow
Would that the meek were no longer mellow
Would that the manager have no one to boss
Would that Christ died not on the Cross

Would that the drummer have nothing to beat
Would that a radiator emit no heat
Would that the jacket have not a pocket
Would that an astronaut have not a rocket
Would that the waiter forget all his orders
Would that the country no longer have borders
Would that a fire give off no smoke
Would that the washer no longer soak
Would that the barman no longer serve beers
Would that the weeper run out of tears
Would that the shrink have no one to judge
Would that the wrestler have no opponent to budge
Would that the guitarist have not a string
Would that the wasp can no longer sting
Would that the champion were no longer best
Would that the sleeper have nowhere to rest
Would that the range be free from balls
Would that the telephonist no longer takes calls
Would that the walls contain no bricks
Would that a dog were all out of licks
Would that the shoes both have no soles
Would that the aspirant have not any goals
Would that the fingers have no more nails
Would that the boats have no more sails
Would that the carpenter run out of wood
Would that the moralist were no longer good
Would that the dentist treat no more teeth
Would that Remembrance Day not include a wreath
Would that the window were no more transparent
Would that the mother were no longer a parent
Would that the beard contain no hairs
Would that the borrower have no more lairs
Would that the monarch have not a subject
Would that the target not be an object

Would that a crossword have not a grid
Would that an auction hold not a bid
Would that a golf course have no more holes
Would that a rink hold not skating or bowls
Would that a toilet receive no more piss
Would that a snake can no longer hiss
Would that a fascist no longer hate
Would that a lover not find a date
Would that a drinker no longer imbibe
Would that a crook not take a bribe
Would that a gay man no longer meet queers
Would that an entertainer no longer hear cheers
Would that a painter no longer see colour
Would that grey clouds no longer be duller
Would that the jails have no more bars
Would that breasts be not held up by bras
Would that the table not have a leg
Would that the homeless need not have to beg
Would that the brothers be not siblings
Would that the obese not partake nibblings
Would that MPs not claim expenses
Would that the lunatic not regain his senses

Would that all of the above be true
Or even just one line
Then the mirrors of consciousness
Would appear for all to view the inner cosmos

Valid Air Tax

I was there
The day they taxed the air
They said it was only fair
To tax the polluted air
The global multinationals
The military–industrial complexes
The remnants of the old 'Economic League'
The monetarist monarchies
The business communities
Couldn't believe they hadn't thought of it sooner
Oxygen, nitrogen and other gases
Would have to be paid for via taxes
There'd be no get-out for each member of the populace
From the remotest island, to the denizens of the metropolis
Who's going to pay for abject acid rain?
Why the plebs of course
Their bank accounts debited, if not now in due course
Twenty pounds a week seemed a fair sum
Opposition protesters were gagged and made dumb
By the use of tasers or else a stun gun
A grand a year – or thereabouts
Lords and ladies exempted – unlike us louts
We were there
The day they taxed the air
They said it was only fair
To tax the polluted air

Drinking and Waiting

Sentimentality is the flip side of aggression
Ninety per cent of the law so-called possession
In a world of soaps, reality TV and tabloid
Thank God for the friendship of the poet Rab Lloyd

The world of sport contains the lowest common denominator
I am a liquid-crystal display residing north of the thermometer
So much useless rubbish and oceans of meaningless words
Even the lowest life form has to avoid the tidal turds

I drink and I wait in lieu of enhancement
Middle age need not be the enemy of advancement
Solitude or company are just like heads or tails
Only the enlightened can sleep on a bed of nails

The discerning man may find in a day what a clot will never see
To praise idleness or embrace the busy bee?
To love is to suffer and its absence much the same
How much that we experience depends on our Christian name

In a world of the bellicose, fascist and bigot
A volcano in an iceberg was the retired Piggott
The pleasures of the damned are a boon to the soul
What happens after the consumption of the breakfast bowl?

A cup of caffeine or else a tube of tobacco
Soy sauce or barbecue not forgetting Tabasco
So here I sit once again with replete glass in hand
Will a metal detector locate a single grain of sand?

Non Sec Whitter

Enter captain's log
Strip the dialogue
Provide the plant with coal
Fill the begging bowl
Relieve the tank of oil
Bring the rice to boil
Shank the shot away
Begin a new day
Sever fickle ties
See the sun arise
Sense impending doom
Clean the rancid room
Adore the splendid silence
Eschew mundane violence
Feel the cooling wind
Upon the face pinned
Contain the feral beast
Observe dilating yeast
Break the stagnant tension
Unknown pleasures mention
Swap your idol for a phantom
The heavyweight's now a bantam
Caress the silky skin
Don't be afraid to win
Roll your rugged rock higher
Beware the untrained flyer
Wash the window with wipers
Avoid the world of diapers
Employ a silver machine
Don't regret what might have been
Drink the contents of a can
Then my boy you'll be
Abolish all ills

In tea dissolve pills
Fill the tank aplenty
Vision twenty-twenty
Relieve the books of the money
Taste tobacco, nicotine and honey
Conclude on a vibrant note
Shelter the migrants' boat

Gerry and Sally Mander

We are all the products of our hard-won failures
Like cycling up on a mountain minus derailleurs
It's not the port you arrive at, it's how you weather the storm
Today's dapper man, may still be forlorn

Good and bad define these terms from somewhere up above
Every hawksian aficionado will terminate as a dove
A driven man always needs a highly skilled chauffeur
The workaholic was once dubbed a lowly billed loafer

Come into my arms and I shall embrace thee
Forget about a single bottle, buy a case of three
I sat on the veranda watching the world fall pass
Every soul needs sustenance, applying to all class

Marriage is a prison, as the golden band is locked
Locked upon the finger as the ship docked
I wish I was a sailor, far away from dry land
The mind of the poet is different from the blithe fan

You may run a rotten borough in a sea of sleaze
If I can shoot rabbits, we can shoot the breeze
It takes years to find the nerve to be apart from the mob
A little knowledge is a curse for each yard of yob

Jesus comes as God is on His way
The long night yields to the dawning day
I got down on my knees in the pew to pray
I implore you now, I beg you to stay

The Sonneteer's Serenade

The reason that I write is not that I'm that good
But so many others are absolutely frigging awful
Every fire needs charcoal or better still hewn wood
So few folks are upstanding and bibulously lawful

There's been no great poet
Since the days of Larkin and Bukowski
If you have a disease then go and throw it
Where's the remote control and that bastard house key?

This collage of crud can drive a man insane
Chain-smoking cigarettes – a way to pass the hours
Another bloody day of high winds and vicious rains
Meet me late at night by the arbour or the bowers

This should be the end of a normal sonnet
But I'll have another verse with no bloody bonnet

Here we go again as sure as Easter is Easter
Thank God for a warm bed and the haven siesta
My bank account appears to have had a stroke
Too many of my friends waste their time snorting coke

Health comes and goes as a hard-on does for love
Each and every hawk ends life as a docile dove
There's only eight more lines before you return to your drinking
Eyelashes the world over work overtime blinking

This visage of vice makes existence worthwhile
Don't believe the myth of existentialism and make mirth mine
The final quatrain is the easiest as the end is nigh
Thank the stars for the National Health Service created by Nye

A million stars may break a dromedary's spine just fine
Balls to your partner and fill up your glasses with wine

There's a Guest in My House

There's a guest in my house
Maybe a burglar or intruder
That lousy liberal louse
Definitely not Pablo Neruda
I'm kissing the big sea
I won't bore you with the details
I never cared for Stevie Nicks see
Where would we be without retail?
So what does one do?
Maybe go back to the world?
In America one can do
As life itself unfurled
All times are pain
All times are pai
All times are pa
All times are p
All times are
All times ar
All times a
All times
All time
All tim
All ti
All t
All
Al
A
Au hazard Russian tsar!
Go bastard rushing car!

Reflections in a Garden High

I sat alone one summer's day in the solace of the garden
As the sun sang out anew and the earth began to harden
The clothes flapped on the washing lines as if flags
As climbers on mountains elsewhere negotiated crags

I placed a glass of cider on the stump of an ancient tree
And safeguarded my sacred drink from the attentions of a bee
I lit another cigarette and the smoke danced as a cloud
The sound of passing vehicles alerted my head bowed

The world itself a gentle place, if only for an hour
Later when I switched on the news life again was sour
An intellect amongst oafs some men sometimes feel
A tiny cog is not lost even within a wheel

Perhaps this will be the first sonnet I ever have published
We all reserve the right to be offended –
but I hope I'm not rubbished

Obituary Attachment

I read a potted history of a life in half a dozen columns
It seems that the deceased was exuberant not solemn
I feel a certain envy at such replete achievement
A shame it was discovered through the process of bereavement
I always note the age – often past threescore and ten
I wish I had known then or at least had a yen
What will be my legacy when I leave this earth?
I hope to leave behind some snippets of worth
A long-forgotten actor or musician has gone
Yet for a term in history their star shone
Someone's death as infotainment – that's how it goes
The late boxing legend survived so many blows
An eventful journey from the crib to the hearse
I thought I'd like to share it via this verse

The Six Things That Grow Buds

The first thing that one needs is a chair to sit in comfort
As the orchestra needs a score, a conductor and a trumpet
The second prerequisite is a pen to set down words
As the ornithologist needs a field glass to watch the birds
The paper is the lucky recipient of the ink that is flowing
Every Gareth Edwards needs a Jacques Fouroux or Sid Going
A large bottle of alcohol will release a world of clarity
To break one through to the other side of parity
'Tobacco aids contemplation' so says Professor Scruton
Not a stodgy meal of meat and two veg and crouton
All the above help to activate the imagination
One may finally come face-to-face with one's destination
Half a dozen things to stoke poetic fires
That's all that creative writing requires

The Climate

The mountain wears a belt of missed in the early morning
As another pauper gathers his effects for the purposes of pawning
Exposed to the elements – within and without
The philistine does not allow himself the luxury of doubt

A rainbow rises over the deceased's apartment
As the mourners return for refreshments with or without partners
The weather changes ten times a day at least in this locale
As the reverent swap their sunglasses for bifocals

Black attracts the heat and may repel marauders
As on TV the militia cross over the rebel borders
Imbibing is a prerequisite in terms of due respect
Let's hope that health and safety do not choose this time to inspect

Old acquaintances are renewed – good, bad and so-so
On occasions such as these you'll need recourse to a yo-yo
A loosening of the ties – temporary and permanent
As some folks look down – others at the firmament

Of course you say the right things – what choice do you have
Every person in a crowd needs a sociable satnav
You take out a cutting from the obituary column
Some relax in drink – others stay quite solemn

Many will forget – at least within a fortnight
The River Lethe welcomes the meek and the forthright
The crowd will start to dwindle after several hours
As inside the edifice you take shelter from the showers

The Seventh Dissipation

I might have been a shroud in silhouette
Drifting like a cloistered cloud in debt
Across vacant skies

I may have been a slatternly sort
Knowing where the gear is bought
Amongst the townsfolk's ties

I could have been a condemned conscript
Remaining always tight-lipped
Amidst the floating folly's flies

I was perhaps a man indigent
Sharpening the spears of trident
For the Lords of war's supplies

I maybe wore an asylum's jacket
Climbing the door and bracket
On the thousandth elevator rise

I felt I was a deposed dictator
Dwelling somewhere near the equator
In the garden of disguise

I knelt to open a cryptic coffin
To find a bloodless boffin
Laughing at the gods of lies

www.ingramcontent.com/pod-product-compliance
Lightning Source LLC
Chambersburg PA
CBHW051848040426
42447CB00006B/744